CRISTIANO RONALDO

THE BOY WHO DREAMED OF BEING A CHAMPION

FROM MADEIRA TO MAGNIFICENCE: A TALE OF PASSION, PERSEVERANCE, AND PRESTIGE

Michael Langdon

itsmikelangdon

Dedication

To Sophie:

Thank you for reigniting that spark within me.

"When you play with Ronaldo on your team, you are already 1-0 up."

Zinedine Zidane

Before you start

This book is produced with 🧡 for children everywhere in the USA.

As it was originally written for a global audience, you will find that we call soccer "football" throughout the book.

Please know that we mean soccer in those instances - the same beautiful game that unites us all.

Table of Contents

INTRODUCTION 15

MADEIRA MAGIC 17

A Star is Born 18

The Spark Within 20

Little Feet, Big Dreams 22

Lisbon's Lessons 24

LIFE IN ENGLAND 27

The Game That Changed Everything 28

CR7 Emerges 30

Maiden Voyage With United 32

Dogged Determination 34

Becoming Unstoppable 36

LIFE IN SPAIN 39

Real's Real Talent 40

Portugal's Prime Man 42

Simply The Best 44

European King 46

Real Madrid Peak 48

LIFE IN ITALY 51

Incredible in Italy 52

Nations League Triumph 54

United U-turn 56

LIFE IN SAUDI ARABIA 59

Saudi Whispers 60

The Record Breaker 62

Evolution of The Best 64

Celebration Icon 66

Greatness From Within 68

Life Outside of Football 70

The Greatest Forever 72

Introduction

People will forever debate who the best football player of all time is.

The likes of Pelé, Marta, Messi, Hamm and Maradona will always be in the mix - often trading places at the top of everyone's list.

Football, a sport played from the heart, can easily be measured with cold, hard stats.

Very few people will ever debate that Cristiano Ronaldo has got the most incredible stats in the history of the sport.

Stats that probably make him the best soccer player ever. Forever.

MADEIRA MAGIC

A Star Is Born

In a little corner of the world, surrounded by the big blue ocean, is a beautiful island named Madeira. This island, nestled in the heart of the Atlantic Ocean, has its closest continent as Africa.

In 1985, within Madeira's capital city of Funchal, a wonderful event took place in February: the birth of a special boy named Cristiano Ronaldo.

Cristiano's life in Madeira was a little bit like a challenging adventure. His mommy, Maria, and his daddy, José, didn't have lots of money to buy toys or fancy clothes, but that didn't stop him from smiling.

His parents worked really hard, with his mom cooking yummy meals and his dad looking after gardens, to make sure Cristiano and his older brothers and sisters were happy and cared for.

Cristiano's dad's favorite actor was a man called Ronald Reagan, and that's why Ronaldo was given his name.

Even though times were sometimes tricky, and new football shoes were a luxury he couldn't always afford, Cristiano's love for football shone brightly. His mommy even used to stitch up his old, worn-out shoes so he could play and laugh and kick the ball under the warm Madeiran sun. His dad introduced him to the exciting world of football, sharing stories and lessons about the sport they both loved so much.

This little boy, with twinkling eyes and an unstoppable spirit, didn't know it yet, but he was taking his first steps towards becoming a hero in the amazing world of soccer, where his tale would be told for generations to come.

And so, the exciting story of Cristiano Ronaldo, the boy from Madeira with big dreams and a gleaming smile, begins...

MADEIRA

The Spark Within

Near the beautiful beaches of Madeira, little Cristiano Ronaldo's love for football kept growing! Imagine being so tiny yet having such a huge dream bubbling inside of you, like a secret you can't wait to share with the world.

When Cristiano was 9 years old, it started becoming increasingly evident that he was very talented. Every day, Cristiano would run outside, a football bouncing at his eager feet, his eyes shining with determination and joy.

The ball wasn't new or shiny, but in Cristiano's eyes, it was the most precious treasure. With every kick, every goal, every little victory in the narrow alleyways with friends, he could feel a special tickle in his heart, whispering promises of big dreams and enchanting adventures ahead.

His parents watched their little boy, with hair as dark as the night and a smile as bright as the day, darting in the wind, and they knew: his passion for the sport was as boundless as the ocean encircling their island home.

In the world of Cristiano's childhood, where every stone and corner became a stadium of dreams, the spark within him grew brighter and warmer. Even when he missed a goal, or his shoes showed new scuffs and tears, his spirit never dimmed. Because Cristiano was not just playing; he was learning, dreaming, and becoming.

Little Feet, Big Dreams

One sunny day, after many games played in the street with his neighborhood friends, a man came to see Cristiano play football.

His name was Aurelio Pereira and he had come all the way from mainland Portugal to see 11-year-old Ronaldo play.

He was very impressed by the young boy he saw on the field, so he offered him a once in a lifetime opportunity. It was an invitation to join a football academy in a bustling city called Lisbon, which was miles and miles away across the vast, twinkling ocean.

While Cristiano's heart raced with excitement, it also weighed heavy with the prospect of missing his dear parents, Maria and José.

At the tender age of 11, Ronaldo's determination and drive were already being put to the test. His eyes gleamed with the thrill of new horizons, yet they also held the moisture of impending goodbyes. Despite his parents wanting him to stay, Cristiano knew he had a chance of becoming a professional football player.

With a suitcase packed with dreams and a tiny lump in his throat, he hugged his parents, promising to make them proud. He was determined to turn all those playful kicks and joyful runs in the narrow streets of Funchal into real-life magic in the big stadiums of mainland Europe.

And so, under the watchful eyes of the Madeira stars, Cristiano sailed towards his big dreams, waving goodbye to his beloved island en route to the bright lights of Lisbon in Portugal.

Lisbon's Lessons

As a 12-year-old boy, Cristiano had a three-day trial with Sporting Football Club in Lisbon.

The club were so impressed with how he played the game that they paid his soccer club in Madeira $2,000 (£1,500) to bring him to Lisbon permanently.

The move brought him to a vibrant city, a stark contrast to the tranquil vibes of Madeira. The sounds of crowded streets, fast-moving cars, and bustling markets were both exciting and a little daunting for the young footballer. Cristiano found himself in a new world, far away from the familiar faces and comforting smiles of home.

Ronaldo, despite being a tiny boy in a giant city, held onto his dreams like a superhero's shield, defending against homesickness and fears.

Sporting Lisbon's football academy eventually became his new home, and his teammates turned into his new family. Every day, he'd lace up his boots, put on his Sporting kit, and with every kick and every goal, he painted his love, his passion for the beautiful game.

Off the field, life wasn't easy for Ronaldo. Often hungry, he would linger near his local McDonald's, hoping for leftover burgers to have for dinner. Little did he know that there was one upcoming game that was about to change his life forever...

reebok

LIFE IN ENGLAND

The Game That Changed Everything

In the summer of 2003, a friendly match was organized between Sporting Lisbon and Manchester United.

A young and relatively unknown 18-year-old Cristiano Ronaldo took the field for Sporting Lisbon and what unfolded in those 90 minutes would become a turning point in football history.

Ronaldo's spellbinding footwork, pace, and skill left both spectators and players utterly astonished. Ronaldo tormented the experienced United defenders, dancing past them with an effortless ease that belied his tender age.

His deft footwork, swift movements, and a dazzling display of skill during the match left the defenders of the esteemed English club chasing shadows.

The Manchester United players joked at full-time that they had to give right back John O'shea medicine because Ronaldo had given him a massive headache! They *begged* United's manager Sir Alex Ferguson to sign him immediately. He was *that* good.

Ferguson went over to the dressing room next door and asked to see Ronaldo.

"How would you like to come and play for Manchester United, Cristiano?" He asked gently.

Ronaldo's heart skipped a beat. Was this a dream? Moving to England meant leaving his beloved Lisbon, but it also meant stepping into a bigger world of football, where he could shine even brighter!

Five days later, a deal to sign Cristiano Ronaldo for Manchester United was agreed.

The little boy from Madeira was on his way to England...

PT
28

CR7 Emerges

Cristiano arrived in England as the most expensive teenager in English football history. Talk about pressure! And the pressure was about to get even bigger...

You see, Cristiano wanted to wear the number 28 shirt, which he had worn at Sporting Lisbon. But in a surprising twist, Sir Alex Ferguson, Manchester United's strict manager, handed him the number 7 shirt instead!

This wasn't just any number. It carried the weight and wonder of the legends who had worn it before for Manchester United. The likes of George Best, Eric Cantona and David Beckham.

Sir Alex saw a future legend in Cristiano and gave him the number to pave a new path in it.

Cristiano's debut for Manchester United came in August 2003 against Bolton Wanderers. After showcasing his skills in that match, the entire stadium gave him a standing ovation. Even George Best, the other legendary number 7 for United, proclaimed it as one of the most thrilling debuts he'd ever seen!

Yet, for all his brilliance, Ronaldo wouldn't net his first goal for the team until November 2003.

But when that goal arrived, it was spectacular! A fierce, curling free-kick against Portsmouth that had fans erupting in celebration.

This marked the beginning of many unforgettable moments in his career.

From there, his journey only gained momentum...

MANCHESTER
UNITED

Maiden Voyage With United

For the remainder of the season, Ronaldo secured his place in the United First Team.

His hard work was paying off, and on May 22 2004, he found himself in the starting line up for The FA Cup final in Cardiff.

The FA Cup is the oldest club competition in the world, and Cristiano Ronaldo, still only a teenager, was not just starting in the final - he was about to create *history* in it.

Our young hero found himself dancing on the pitch that day, gliding past every tackle that the Millwall defenders would throw at him.

They thought they had managed to stop him in the first half, but a minute before the whistle went, Ronaldo rose high in the box to head a rocket of a header into the back of the net.

This teenager had just announced himself on the world stage!

An hour later, and after two more goals scored by United, he found himself celebrating a victory, with The FA Cup held high above his head!

His crucial goal in the final against Millwall, and the persistent, electrifying performances throughout the season played a key role in leading the team to FA Cup glory in his inaugural season in England.

This marked his first English trophy, and it was merely the beginning! He had undoubtedly captured the hearts of United fans everywhere.

And so, the boy from Madeira began building his legacy, stitch by stitch, in a red shirt, under the gleaming English lights.

Dogged Determination

Ronaldo made his debut for Portugal in a game against Kazakhstan in 2003.

By the time the 2006 World Cup came round he had already become the first name on the team sheet. However, that World Cup presented him with one of his most challenging moments in England.

During the World Cup in Germany, an incident in a game between Portugal and England put Cristiano in a tricky spot. His friend, Wayne Rooney, who was also his teammate at Manchester United, was involved in a tangle on the pitch.

Cristiano was caught in a situation where he had to choose between being a good friend or doing anything to try and win for his country. He chose the latter, and was seen urging the referee to take action against Wayne.

This moment led to lots of boos and frowns aimed at Ronaldo when he got back to playing in England. He asked Alex Ferguson to be transferred, but the manager decided to stand by him and told him to be strong. After all, good guys always win.

In the season that followed, Cristiano played with a kind of magic that quickly turned those boos into cheers and made the frowning faces light up with smiles again.

His dedication and incredible skills led Manchester United to winning the Premier League title in 2007! And in doing so he broke the 20 goal barrier in one season for the first time in his career.

It was a special moment when he lifted his first Premier League trophy. It was a symbol of the storms he'd weathered. He showed everyone that no matter how bumpy the journey gets, hard work pays off.

BARCLAYS
BARCLAYS
BARCLAYS

Becoming Unstoppable

The following season, Ronaldo sky-rocketed into football greatness!

His speedy legs and direct football wreaked havoc on every defence he came across. He finished the 2007-2008 season scoring a jaw-dropping 42 goals!

The absolute highlight of that season was the 2008 UEFA Champions League Final against Chelsea. 26 minutes into the final in Moscow, Ronaldo jumped higher than the Chelsea defence, and headed the ball into the goal, giving Manchester United a vital lead.

Even though he missed a penalty later on, United won the game in the end, and Ronaldo got his first Champions League title! People all over the world were now aware of his amazing skills, and he was named the FIFA World Player of the Year in 2008.

The following season, whispers off the field about Ronaldo possibly leaving Manchester United started buzzing around. That didn't stop being awesome on the field, scoring 26 goals and helping his team win another Premier League title.

United made it to the Champions League final again, however, this time they lost the final to Barcelona (who at the time, had possibly the best team the world has *ever* seen!)

In June 2009, Ronaldo was transferred to Real Madrid in Spain for a record-breaking $100 million! (£80 million) Wearing the white jersey of Real Madrid, his world legacy was about to get even bigger!

RONALDO
7
10
5

LIFE IN SPAIN

Real's Real Talent

Oh, what an exciting time it was for Cristiano Ronaldo between 2009 and 2013! His football superpowers exploded when he moved to the most famous team in the world!

In the first four years of donning the famous white jersey of Real Madrid, Cristiano scored an astonishing 201 goals. Imagine that – 201 times the ball hit the back of the net all because of him!

At the end of the 2011 season, Ronaldo and his teammates lifted the Copa del Rey trophy, which is a HUGE deal in Spain.

What made it even a bigger deal is that they won the final against their biggest rivals, Barcelona.

Remember that Barcelona had arguably the best team in the world at the time? A team that included Lionel Messi?

Well, Ronaldo's powerful headed goal was the only one in the match, making Real Madrid the champions!

On the international level, one of Cristiano's most heart-touching moments happened in 2012 whilst he was playing for Portugal in the European Championship.

Now wearing his favored number 7 shirt for his country too, and entrusted with the captain's armband, he led his team all the way to the finals!

Cristiano's performances were breathtaking and he managed to become the top scorer of the tournament with 3 goals to his name.

Sadly, Portugal went on to lose on penalties in the semi-final against Spain. It was very hard for Ronaldo to take that loss - he was distraught that day.

bwi

Portugal's Prime Man

Ronaldo went from strength to strength after that semi-final defeat to Spain, and only a few months later he became one of the youngest players in history to reach 100 games for their country.

He was on a quest to win an international tournament with his beloved Portugal. And in one of Cristiano's most unforgettable matches, he sent Portugal to the 2014 World Cup.

In a crucial play-off game against Sweden, he scored an astounding hat-trick, pretty much carrying the Portuguese all the way to Brazil 2014.

This game was also viewed as a face-off between two of the era's greatest footballers: Cristiano Ronaldo and Zlatan Ibrahimovic. Thanks to Ronaldo's three goals, he not only outshone Ibrahimovic but also ensured his nation's spot in the World Cup.

Ronaldo, still only in his twenties, became Portugal's all-time top scorer en route to Brazil 2014!

Sadly, the South American World Cup exposed the Portuguese weaknesses and showed that they couldn't rely only on Ronaldo to win a trophy. They were eliminated in the first round and the team endured one of the toughest times in their history.

But, as the saying goes, when the going gets tough, the tough get going. And that's exactly what Cristiano did.

He buckled down, worked hard, and qualified his team for the European Championships of 2016 which were being held in France.

Simply The Best

Cristiano experienced some of his best years at club level between 2013 and 2016.

In 2013 and 2014, he was voted the world's best player, largely due to his remarkable accomplishments with Real Madrid.

The crowning achievement came in 2014 when he helped Real Madrid clinch the Champions League title. The club hadn't won this trophy for 12 long years, and for a team as successful as Real Madrid, that felt like an eternity!

Cristiano played a pivotal role in ending this wait. In the dramatic 2014 Champions League final, he scored a crucial penalty against their city rivals, Atletico Madrid. The joy of this moment was so immense that he couldn't resist tearing off his shirt in celebration!

By then, Cristiano had not only become Real Madrid's all-time top scorer but had also forged an intense rivalry with Lionel Messi. The two of them stood out as the finest footballers in the world, demonstrating skills that had never before been seen.

For an entire decade, from 2008 to 2017, the title of the best footballer of the year was passed between these two legends.

But in 2016, Cristiano did something so extraordinary that many believed it didn't just secure his status as the best player of the year, but also placed him a notch above Lionel Messi...

7
13

European King

Many football experts and fans often said that what might distinguish Messi and Ronaldo would be winning an international tournament with their respective countries.

While both players showcased breathtaking skills at the club level, their performances for their national teams didn't quite match those highs. Well, in 2016 that all changed.

Ronaldo's incredible skills and leadership helped Portugal reach the final of Euro 2016. The final was in Paris, on a warm July evening, and Portugal kicked off the game - Ronaldo ready to make history.

However, life had a twist in store for him. In the first half of the game against France, he got injured and had to leave the field in tears. It was heartbreaking for him and his fans.

But champions don't give up that easily! Ronaldo turned into the team's biggest cheerleader, motivating his teammates from the sidelines.

Portugal fought with all their hearts, and in the end, a player named Éder scored the winning goal in extra time! Portugal won the Euros, and Ronaldo's dream of bringing glory to his country came true!

This victory was a game-changer for Ronaldo. It showed that he wasn’t just a great player; he was a leader who could inspire his team to triumph even when he couldn’t play. His impact on the Portuguese side that summer was like magic. He didn't just win a trophy; he won the hearts of millions and cemented his place among the all-time greats of soccer.

At that time, many critics started to agree that Ronaldo was in fact the undoubted G.O.A.T. (Greatest Of All Time).

UEFA EURO
UEFA EURO
7

Real Madrid Peak

While many people tend to relax once they've reached their goals, Ronaldo is not your average person. Instead, he pressed on even harder after leading Portugal to victory in Euro 2016!

In 2018 Ronaldo helped Real Madrid win the Champions league for a third consecutive time. Winning the Champions League three times in a row is an incredible achievement in the modern game, but more impressively, in doing so, Ronaldo became the first player *ever* to win the competition 5 times.

The most unforgettable moment in winning his 5th Champions League medal happened when Real Madrid faced Juventus in the quarter finals. During this match, Ronaldo pulled off something truly magical. A move so brave and audacious that it will be forever remembered as one of the greatest goals ever!

His teammate passed him the ball slightly too high and too far back for Ronaldo to be able to control it, let alone kick it. But in the blink of an eye, Ronaldo soared into the air, twisting and contorting his body, and then, with his back to goal and whilst floating 2 meters up in the air - BOOM!

The ball rocketed into the back of the net. He had just scored the most beautiful bicycle kick!

Everyone watching went wild. It was a work of art on the football field. Ronaldo ended that game with two goals and one assist.

Replays of that incredible goal were watched over and over again all over the world. People couldn't stop talking about the goal, especially the people who owned Juventus, the Italian club he had just scored against...

RONALD
2
LUCAS V
17

LIFE IN ITALY

Incredible In Italy

Three months after scoring that goal against Juventus, Cristiano Ronaldo packed his bags and set off on a new adventure to Italy, to join none other than Juventus themselves!

He scored his first two goals for Juventus in a match against Sassuolo. His second goal was extra special because it marked his 400th goal in a league match. What a milestone!

Ronaldo won the Scudetto in his first season with Juventus. The Scudetto is the affectionate name Italians give to the Serie A league winners.

In winning it, he became the first player to win league titles in the three major European Leagues (The English Premier League, Spain's La Liga and Italy's Serie A).

He was also voted Serie A's best player in his first season in Italy. It would seem that anywhere Ronaldo went, there was just no stopping him!

One of his most incredible moments in a Juventus shirt, and one of the most amazing things ever seen on a soccer field, happened on December 18 2019 against Sampdoria.

In an effort to reach a ball lofted high into the opposition's box, Ronaldo jumped to a height of 2.57 meters (that's higher than the crossbar!) to head the winning goal.

Cristiano ended the season with 37 goals in all competitions for Juventus; a number which saw him break Felice Borel's club record of 36 goals in a single season. A record that had stood for over 80 years!

Most players start slowing down at 34 years of age. Ronaldo however, was busy breaking records that had stood for decades!

Jeep
15
29
15

Nations League Triumph

As Cristiano conquered every challenge faced at club level, 2019 brought a different challenge on the international front.

UEFA had just introduced a new tournament for the top soccer nations in Europe. It was called the Nations League and Ronaldo began this journey by scoring a hat-trick against Switzerland in the semi-finals to guide his beloved Portugal to the final.

In the grand finale, Portugal clashed with the Netherlands. The stadium was buzzing with excitement, and fans from around the world tuned in.

The match was intense, with both teams fighting hard for victory. As always, Ronaldo, with the captain's armband wrapped around his arm, led his team using his experience and talent...

Portugal won the game 1-0.

After the final whistle, Ronaldo lifted the new Nations League trophy, and the celebrations were a sight to behold!

It was a moment of pride and joy for Ronaldo and his teammates. They had just won the very first Nations League!

By September 2020 he had scored more than 100 goals for Portugal and over 700 career goals for club and country!

Ronaldo was undoubtedly still one of the global soccer superstars, showing that, unlike many other soccer legends, age was not going to slow him down!

RESPECT

United U-turn

In the summer of 2021, Manchester United announced that they had agreed to bring Ronaldo back to the team. United fans couldn't believe their eyes - one of the greatest ever players to don the United shirt was coming back!

And guess what? Ronaldo was going to wear the number 7 shirt once again! Edinson Cavani, another fantastic player at United, kindly agreed to switch to number 21, allowing Ronaldo to have his favorite number back.

When the news broke, fans rushed to get their hands on Ronaldo's new Manchester United jersey. It was so popular that it broke all-time records for shirt sales in the first 24 hours.

It even surpassed the sales of Messi shirts when he moved to Paris Saint-Germain. That's how excited everyone was to see Ronaldo back in the red and white jersey!

Ronaldo began his season back in Manchester with two debut goals against Newcastle United. As the season went on, Ronaldo continued to show his magic on the field.

He kept breaking records too, becoming the first player to score in five consecutive matches of a Champions League campaign for an English club!

Ronaldo ended the season with 24 goals. Considering he was 37 and playing in one of the world's toughest leagues, this feat was truly extraordinary. He was even selected for the Premier League Team of the Year.

While he had personal success, United finished in sixth place and didn't win any trophies. But the fans knew that with Ronaldo back, the future held the promise of greatness once again.

TeamViewer

LIFE IN SAUDI ARABIA

Saudi Whispers

Sometimes, things take an unexpected turn, even for soccer legends like Cristiano Ronaldo.

After feeling increasingly unhappy with Manchester United, Ronaldo looked for a new beginning. He expressed feeling "betrayed" by some individuals at Manchester United and openly admitted his lack of respect for their manager, Erik Ten Hag.

Ronaldo's frustrations came from his belief that the club hadn't evolved much since the glory days of the iconic manager, Sir Alex Ferguson. He felt that the Glazer family, the owners of Manchester United, could be doing a better job of running the club.

Eventually, Ronaldo and United decided it was best to part ways, mutually agreeing to terminate his contract.

Ronaldo wasn't one to dwell on the past. He represented Portugal in the World Cup held in Qatar, although they were sadly knocked out in the Quarter Final by Morocco.

However, Ronaldo's soccer story was far from its final chapter. On December 30, 2022, he signed a deal with Saudi Arabian club Al Nassr.

Ronaldo's new contract was something special, making him the highest-paid soccer player in history! His salary was a whopping $200 million per year (£175m).

Ronaldo was ready for a new adventure in a new country, and soccer fans around the world, and especially in the Middle East, were eager to see what he would achieve with Al Nassr.

The Record Breaker

As Ronaldo continues to break records in Saudi Arabia, it is clear that there isn't a player on Earth that has, or will ever have, more impressive stats. Especially when it comes to international football.

At the time of writing this book, Cristiano is still playing for Portugal, racking up an impressive 202 international appearances.

More than anyone in the world.

It is worth pointing out that the probability of another player crossing the 200-appearance mark, like Cristiano has, is very unlikely.

In 2021, Portugal played against the Republic of Ireland in a World Cup qualifier at Estádio Algarve. That day, Ronaldo was a man on a mission. He netted two extraordinary headers.

Those two goals weren't just any goals. They allowed Ronaldo to leap past Ali Daei's long-held world record, crowning him the sole record holder for the most international goals by a male player. Those were his 110th and 111th international goals!

At the time of writing, he has scored 125 times for his country.

More than anyone in the world.

Lionel Messi is the only active player who's on course to emulate this achievement, and he's still "only" on 104 goals - so unlikely to match Cristiano's record.

At the time of writing (late 2023), he has scored more goals in 2023 than any other player on earth - and he's almost 39 years old!

RESPECT

Evolution Of The Best

Ronaldo's ability to amass such incredible stats is because of his ability to learn, grow and adapt as a football player.

The game in 2023 is played differently to how it was played when he first broke through as a professional in 2003. Ronaldo has adapted his game with each passing season to become the best player he can be.

Back in the early days of his career, Ronaldo was a young winger with Sporting and Manchester United. He played on the right side, and excelled at dribbling and fancy footwork, including his famous step-overs and 'chops,' which wowed fans worldwide.

During his peak at Manchester United, Ronaldo transformed into a prolific goal-scorer, capable of finding the back of the net from anywhere on the field, including set-pieces.

As Ronaldo moved to Real Madrid, his role evolved yet again. He played as a center forward, making clever runs into the penalty area, scoring goals and drawing defenders out of position to create space for his teammates. He was not just a goal-scorer but also an effective creator.

Then came his time at Juventus where he continued to evolve, playing various attacking roles under different managers, from a lone striker to his trademark left-wing position. He dropped deep to receive the ball and became more involved in the build-up.

This evolution has also been seen in the Portugal team, where Ronaldo's ability to adapt and reinvent himself on the field showcase his incredible soccer intelligence and work ethic. He isn't just a player; he is a soccer genius, always finding new ways to contribute to his team's success.

vodafone

Celebration Icon

There are very few players on earth who can influence global culture at the scale at which Cristiano Ronaldo has. Putting aside his incredible skills on the soccer field; he also had some of the most famous goal celebrations in the game. These celebrations were like his own special way of saying, "I did it!"

The celebrations have filtered through school playgrounds in every corner of the world. With millions of children imitating their hero after scoring in their local games.

One celebration that got everyone talking was during Ronaldo's second spell at Manchester United, where he would interlock his fingers after scoring a goal and pretend he was meditating.

However, there was one celebration that was truly iconic and had children and adults all over the world imitating it. After scoring a goal, Ronaldo would jump up high, like he was trying to touch the sky. Then, he would turn in mid-air and land with his legs apart, like a superhero sticking a perfect landing. It was a powerful and dynamic move that showed his strength and agility.

As he landed, Ronaldo would strike his signature power stance, showing off his muscles and his determination. At the same time, he would shout, "Sí," which means "yes" in Spanish and Italian.

This celebration became famous in every country on earth. Every time Ronaldo did the 'Sii', fans in the stadium would cheer, and people watching on TV would smile and clap. It was a moment of pure joy and excitement.

Ronaldo's celebrations were not just about showing off; they were about sharing his passion for the game with the world. They were a reminder that soccer is not just a sport; it's a way to express yourself and have fun.

RONALDO
7
14

Greatness From Within

Ronaldo's outstanding career has been down to his incredible determination to be the very best. This includes practicing on the training ground but also the incredible work he does off the pitch in keeping his body fit.

Ronaldo trains rigorously five days a week for 3 to 4 hours, combining weight training and fitness training.

It wasn't all plain sailing though, when Cristiano was young, he was diagnosed with a heart condition that made his heart beat irregularly.

Most people might have given up on their dreams, but after undergoing surgery and recovering, Cristiano was back on the field, chasing his dreams.

Ronaldo even made headlines at Euro 2020 by removing Coca-Cola bottles during a press conference and encouraging people to drink water instead. He really is all about being healthy!

Ronaldo's influence extends to his teammates too. When he's around, they avoid desserts like apple crumble and custard. They instead choose to have healthier desserts.

Ronaldo treats his body like a temple, and he credits his longevity to fresh and natural foods. He is definitely the type of person who loves his vegetables!

Life Outside Of Football

Ronaldo is a family man and has five children! Yes, you heard that right, five! He's not just a champion on the football pitch; he's also a champion dad. Imagine having Ronaldo as your dad; you'd probably have some amazing soccer genes!

His impact goes beyond the soccer fields. In 2016, after Portugal's big win at Euro 2016, something incredible happened. Remember his hometown Funchal in the island of Madeira?

Well, they gave their airport a new name and it was renamed the Cristiano Ronaldo International Airport. Can you imagine having an airport named after you?

Every single person who now comes to the island will always think of Cristiano as soon as they land. It shows just how much he means to the people of Madeira and Portugal.

In 2007, a Madeira football club called C.D. Nacional decided to honor Ronaldo in a special way. They renamed their youth campus to Cristiano Ronaldo Campus Futebol, a place where young soccer talents can learn and grow, just like Ronaldo did.

And that's not the end of his legacy. In 2013, Ronaldo opened a museum in Funchal called Museu CR7. This museum is not just any museum; it's a place where all his trophies and memorabilia are displayed for everyone to see.

So, whether it's his amazing family, the airport named after him, the youth campus, or the museum, Cristiano Ronaldo's impact goes far beyond the soccer field. He's a true legend both in the game and in the hearts of people all around the world.

Next time your parents ask where you want to go on holiday it might be worth mentioning Madeira so that you can go and see all the incredible sights that made Ronaldo who he is today!

The Greatest Forever

Despite Ronaldo nearing the end of his playing career, it is not too early to say that he's perhaps the finest footballer our planet has ever witnessed.

At the very least, experts universally rank him among the top four maestros of the sport, alongside Pelé, Maradona, and Messi.

But one distinction is clear: Ronaldo's statistics are unmatched.

Ronaldo scores goals like no one else. He's shattered records and netted more than 700 goals in his career! From jaw-dropping free-kicks to powerful headers, he can score in countless ways.

Ronaldo has won seven league titles and the UEFA Champions League five times! His winning mentality and leadership inspire teammates to greatness. No one has ever won more Champions Leagues than him.

He has also conquered the Premier League, La Liga, and Serie A, which are the toughest leagues globally. He's like a conqueror of soccer worlds!

Cristiano is a master of all soccer arts. His dribbling, precision passes, and incredible speed leave defenders in awe. He's a wizard with the ball, creating magic on the field, and mesmerizing millions around the world.

More than an international icon, he is a national hero too! As the commander-in-chief of Portugal, he led them to victory in Euro 2016, their first major international title, and also the Nations League in 2019.

In the epic tale of soccer history, Cristiano Ronaldo stands tall as the greatest hero from the sport. His hard work and adaptability have helped him maintain his status as world no1 for close to two decades!

Not only that, but he's an inspiration to millions of children across the world. A true role model who shows that hard work can turn any dream into reality.

FIFA
FIFA

Made in the USA
Las Vegas, NV
19 February 2025

303d3f0b-4441-42e7-a103-2b74c12e137eR01